CH00847743

Retail Fashion Product Storage and Logistics

by

Charles Nesbitt

ISBN

Also by Charles Nesbitt

FUNDAMENTALS FOR SUCCESSFUL AND SUSTAINABLE FASHION BUYING AND MERCHANDISING

*

FUNDAMENTALS FOR FASHION RETAIL STRATEGY PLANNING AND IMPLEMENTATION

*

FUNDAMENTALS FOR FASHION RETAIL ARITHMETIC, ASSORTMENT PLANNING AND TRADING

*

FUNDAMENTALS OF FASHION RETAIL, TECHNOLOGY, MANUFACTURING AND SUPPLIER MANAGEMENT

*

THE COMPLETE JOURNAL OF FASHION RETAIL BUYING AND MERCHANDISING

*

RETAIL FASHION MERCHANDISE ASSORTMENT PLANNING AND TRADING

3

*

RETAIL FASHION PROCUREMENT TEAM ROLES AND PROCESSES

*

RETAIL FASHION ARITHMETIC

*

RETAIL FASHION SUPPLIER MANAGEMENT

*

RETAIL FASHION SCENARIO AND STRATEGY PLANNING

*

RETAIL FASHION MANUFACTURING AND TECHNOLOGY

*

RETAIL FASHION DATA MANAGEMENT

Table of Contents

PREFACE

The process of buying and selling in some form or other of goods has been with us since time immemorial. Often when one stands in bewilderment in an elegant shopping mall and wonder how all the stores are able to effectively seduce the many shoppers trawling the wide corridors to readily part with their well-earned money while at the same time enabling them to possibly enjoy a wonderful social experience.

The plan of offering goods to the potential customer is a complicated one and is a science that involves many players whose individual contributions slot seamlessly together and are so perfectly co-ordinated that it provides the perception that it is the result of one individual concerted effort.

It will be illustrated as to how the relationships of the major functions that intertwine from the conceptualisation of a product through to the presentation of a finished garment with particular focus on the logistical arm of the business.

The book endeavours to try and outline the basic key principles and mechanisms by which this happens and should be helpful to students, people in retailing and those who are maybe considering a career in the industry. For those who already are part of the fashion buying and merchandising community this book will be beneficial in that it provides a complete simplified overview of all the integral activities and roles that go to make up the topic and thereby will provide a broader insight into their own career.

The material of the book, other than that specifically referenced is the result of the author's own exposure to the subject during a career spanning thirty five years at a major retail organisation in Southern Africa, the support from colleagues, mentors, interaction with suppliers and own research. There has been some cross referencing to other books or technical material but the book focuses largely at a higher level on the key principles, concepts and theories and hence there is none or very little mention of retailers by name or technological packages for some key activities such as planning, allocating, critical path management, logistics and the like.

The fundamental purpose is therefore to provide the basic background that goes into the operational and technical aspects which can be universally applied. While there is merit and great benefits in the use of sophisticated technical packages that live off a common database and also integrate with one another, sadly often the prime emphasis becomes more one of mastering the system and promotes the tendency to live in a silo environment. As a result the importance tends to be focused on that single facet that the system serves rather than the broader picture. The fact that there is a relatively limited amount of material that generally describes the practice commonly known as retailing as an end to end process considering the enormous size of the industry is one of the motivating reasons for the documentation of this book.

INTRODUCTION

Retailing

Retailing is the offer of goods or services for sale by individuals or businesses to an end user. The channels by which these goods reach the final user may vary considerably and arrive via different sources such as wholesalers, trading houses or directly from the manufacturer and there are equally many differing variants in the way the goods are put on sale. Historically it is more likely that shopping would have been done at the village or town market, in a high street shop or at the "mom and pop" store which evolved over time into mass retailing stores that are often housed in shopping malls supported by smaller line shops.

More recently with the advent of the computer utilising various platforms such as the internet or social networks, shopping on line is growing exponentially using electronic payment methods with delivery via the post or with a courier man knocking on the front door of the customer bearing their purchase relatively shortly after the transaction has been processed.

The products that are put on offer will be determined by the demand to satisfy a need in the market place. Broadly the merchandise may be categorized into food stuffs, hard or durable goods such as appliances, furniture and electronics and soft goods that have a limited life span typically clothing, apparel and fabrics. Whatever the nature of the product, the key objective will be to acquire and sell the product at a price that will be more than it cost to bring it to the place of offer and thereby make a profit.

Supporting activities such as the storage, movement of the goods, technology, and marketing will endeavour to ensure that the form, function and profit objective is maximised.

In an effort to put in perspective the activities and interaction between the various functional players and their dependency and integration with each other for the end to end process of the product workflow is broadly depicted in the diagram below

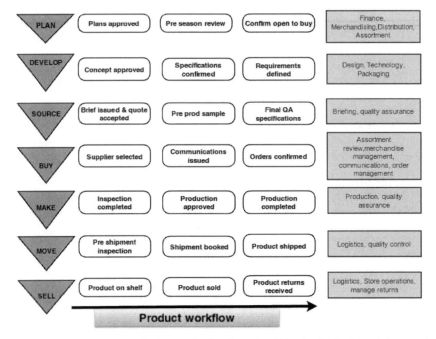

The distinction between supply chain and value chain should be clarified in that it is frequently misunderstood and the interpretation is varied.

Simply put, supply chain is the processes and activities that take place from conceptualisation of styles through to the procurement of raw materials and production process to the logistical operations and the eventual delivery to the end user. The value chain component is the inclusion of those functions that support the supply chain process such as the marketing philosophies. Human resource management, and consultancy resources.

The intimate details of the roles will be exposed in the future chapters as the science of retailing is explored in greater detail.

The retail players

The saying "no man is an island" holds true in many spheres and this is certainly the case in the world of clothing retailing.

Various players, each with very different specialised skills are amalgamated together to deliver a completed outcome which is that of presenting product for sale to potential customers. These players are often very diverse not only in the activities that they perform but also in their personality traits which they possess. The key to a successful team is how maturely the interaction takes place and the mutual respect that every member has for each other's roles.

Below is a brief synopsis of the main player's roles and their dependency and integration with each other. The intimate details of the roles will be exposed in the future chapters as the science of retailing is explored in greater detail.

THE PROCUREMENT TEAM

The foremost players in the clothing and apparel procurement team consist typically of the following members and are described in broad terms.

Designers

Designers have a deep insight into the market they are targeting through the analysis of the changing trends and use these to provide creative direction and develop product designs for the buying teams to consider.

Usually these participants tend to think out of the box and their creative minds can challenge some of the comfort zones of other team members. What must be kept top of mind is that they need to consistently apply their intellect way ahead of time as to what they think the customer requires as opposed to their personal desires.

Typically the character traits which they will possess are that they are independent, spontaneous, extroverts, driven by ideas and are confident by nature.

Although the general perception of the word "designer" conjures up a vision of those who work at couture level, the reality is that it also includes those who are involved in creating ranges which may also be exclusive but will be more widely available and therefore can be considered as having been mass produced. Their choices will be influenced by the type of retailer they work for or the product category that they design for. The more traditional retailer which serves predominantly mature customers will be less influenced by radical fashion swings which in contrast will definitely affect the younger market's high fashion boutiques more rigorously.

Work is done at times under enormous pressure to meet critical deadlines, tough meeting schedules and involves frequent international travel. It is not surprising the perception is often one that they live a life of glory and glamour but contrary to this belief the reality is that it is not as extravagant as made out to be.

The fashion and trade shows, whether they be for yarn, fabric or garments are tiring affairs requiring hard work and stamina as is the shopping for appropriate samples, researching fashion magazines, the use of forecasting trend agencies, internet and blogs and out of all of this they need to possess the ability to then distil the emerging trends to create a storybook that will best suit their organisation's customer profiles.

The designer lives with the constant strain of knowing that their level of success will be measured by the eventual amount of money rung up at the till and getting the styling direction wrong or overextending the life of a particular look could have severe financial implications, especially in the cases where volumes are high.

The real challenge is to convince the buying teams and senior management to buy into their vision and have the confidence that what they have in mind will be commercially acceptable to the customer. The designer cannot ignore the technical aspects of the garment production as many problems can be evaded if these are taken cognisance of during the design process.

Retailers in the southern hemisphere do have the advantage that their seasons follow those of countries in the northern hemisphere which allows them to tap into the more successful designs that are trading in volume. However, with globalisation this is not always as clear cut as it was in previous years and the ability to follow as close to the season as possible requires techniques that facilitates the shortening of lead times and attempt to get the product to market as quickly as possible. The advent of communication technologies such as satellite television, internet and social media have brought exposure to different cultures, sports, films, lifestyles and trends such as those generated by specific events, health drives, environmental awareness and technology platforms that can have significant impacts on fashion which sometimes happen at very short notice.

A very important aspect is that the designer must adhere strictly to, is that of copyright. Instances have occurred that other competitor's garments are copied almost identically whether it be by style, print or design. Invariably the driving reason for this is the speed of being able to turn on a replica at a cheaper price. Although it may not be practical to register and copyright every design, any infringement can still be challenged and a consequence could occur of having the offending garments being removed from display and destroyed.

Buyers
The buyer needs to have a clear understanding of the product that is required which is in line with the trend guidelines best suited to their target customer profiles, for both the high fashion segment as well as those that best serve the more traditional customer.

It is a fact is that the role of the designer and the buyer may be a bit blurred in that they research the same fashion forecasting sites and other sources of inspiration in order to put a range of garments together. Both roles must be aware of sizing, quality and costs related to fabrics, trimmings and production. To achieve this successfully they must be flexible enough to develop and buy the most suitable product that is in line with the prescribed strategy and achieves the desired profit margin in keeping with the set down targets. The evaluation of competitive activity and product ranges through regular store visits and comparative shopping provides the knowledge required to keep ahead of the field.

Effective communication and presentation skills are a prerequisite to brief and interact with suppliers as well as presenting product reviews to colleagues within their own group at all levels of seniority. With this comes the need to be able to accept criticism and resolve problems in a mature manner. The sad fact is that frequently when the analysis of the success of the range is evaluated at the end of the season, if the results are disappointing it is not uncommon for the buyer to shoulder the emotional burden of the poor performance. The truth of the matter is that the range was presented on more than one occasion to all team players including senior management all of whom signed the range off but in the final analysis they are more often than not, as is human nature, reluctant to be accept any proper accountability.

Coupled to ability to understand the wants of the customer is the sourcing of the most suitable supplier that will be selected for the specified product types in terms of their particular skills, technical ability, costing efficiency, attitude, transparency, honesty, focus on quality, communications and competitiveness while still meeting the ethical criteria that are acceptable to society.

A large part of the task will be to maintain good relations with suppliers, while at the same time being able to assertively negotiate prices with them and make sure the planned stocks are delivered on time. Communications need to be clear and specific to avoid disputes over issues which may arise through vague and confusing messages. For these reasons they need to be confident, take decisions based on results and be driven by a sense of urgency.

The buyer has to be multi-talented in that as well as being creative they also need to monitor the sales objectively and be flexible enough to react accordingly in terms of turning on or turning off production and transferring fabric and components to more appealing product styles where sales performance and fast emerging trends dictate.

What is key to be a successful buyer is the ability to work as part of the overall team and influence the rest of the team's activities which could be in the form of a managerial and developmental capacity that could also include both their peers and superiors.

The display of emotional maturity and commercial acumen within the controlled parameters as set by the merchandising arm in terms of the budgets, the number of product options and display space constraints is absolutely essential.

The same principle applies to the relationships that need to be maintained with the technical teams in regard to the use of the most appropriate fabrics which meet the product form and function demands in addition to ensuring that the brand standards of the garment are observed.

The fact that potentially the buyer together with the other retail players will be dealing with three to four seasons simultaneously at different stages for each season makes their task even more complicated. To clarify the phenomenon a bit further, the journey of this book attempts to describe the process from beginning to end for one season but while trading in the current season the thoughts and strategies are being developed and documented for two or possibly three seasons ahead followed by the range development leading up to the production taking place for next upcoming season.

The ability to absorb and interpret vast amounts of information from various sources, much of which originates from complex IT systems, can present a challenge to those who are not analytically minded. Systems have altered the scope of the traditional buyer from being a pure "touchy feely art skill" to having to develop basic technical abilities through the continual emergence of innovative systems which have become a great advantage to the role.

Some buyer's, such as those for knitwear, ladies structured underwear, tailoring and footwear will require more expert fabric and garment construction knowledge of their respective industries in comparison to individuals who select the more straightforward cut, make and trim products such as dresses, blouses and casual trousers.

As the trade environment has become more global and through information technology development it is much faster, interactive and has enabled business to be done more effortlessly from a home base interacting with many different countries. A great deal of the job is done amongst many new emerging countries which has led to a need for urgency and nimbleness in order to locate the most effective plants that meet the quality requirements, be able to assess the required technical abilities, understand the economic and cultural demands of the respective countries as well as the logistical peculiarities and government regulations that may exist.

The sourcing of production has to take on different approaches as the pros and cons of dealing internationally needs to be carefully weighed up against those of dealing with the ever diminishing number of local suppliers. A critical factor is that suppliers must be ethical in terms of labour practices, remuneration, waste management, working conditions and safety. If such conditions are not met it is counter to the interests of the retailer to be associated with such suppliers from both a moral point of view and the exposure of malpractices could lead to negative media reports and the retailer will suffer the consequences that accompany such deeds. The measurement of performance is therefore key to gauging the effectiveness of suppliers.

In larger organisations a buyer will probably be supported by an assistant or trainee buyer who will normally be a person who wishes to pursue a career in the field. They will be largely responsible for the organisation of the ranges, perform some clerical work whilst preparing products for garment reviews, monitoring the product development critical path and production milestones, liaising with suppliers and technology as well as deputising for the buyer when they are out of the office.

A point to note is that the relationship between buyers and suppliers often develops into more than a pure business association due to the fact that they spend much time travelling together and working closely with one another building ranges. Close familiar relationships frequently make it difficult to maintain a business like association for the mutual benefit of both parties and can cloud business decision making and judgment. The temptation of bribery and incentives in exchange for placing large orders may be desirous. For newer naïve buyers the rule that the supplier is not your friend should be firmly applied simply because they are more easily seduced by grandiose lunches and gifts as many have unfortunately found out the hard way when they move on and are no longer of great importance to the particular supplier.

A way of balancing the workloads or ranking of buyers and merchandisers is to evaluate the actual number of suppliers, stock keeping units or barcodes being handled by each buyer and then make comparisons regarding workload and productivity of each buyer to established benchmarks.

Merchandisers

There is a novelty t-shirt on the market which has the following statement blazon across the front panel which reads as follows – *"Merchandise Planner – we do precision guesswork based on unreliable data by those of questionable knowledge".* Although the humour can be appreciated it should be known that this statement is not too far from the truth as the success of merchandising objectives is reliant on many diverse inputs.

The merchandiser or planner applies their focus on maximising profitability from the business end. This is done largely through the analysis of historical sales and the influence of the trend direction to determine the range categories and product breakdown within the overall sales budget.

The role defines what stock levels are required to meet the preset targets such as seasonal stock turnover or forward stock covers based on the sales trends over time. Knowing these requirements, the merchandiser will determine what intake or purchase quantities are needed at any point in time in the season for the total department and each product category.

The level of the budgets will determine the quantity of options in relation to styling, colour palette, size spans, pricing structure and levels of quality per category that will best service the customer for the time that the goods are expected be on offer prior to a new variety of product being introduced in line with the strategic predetermined seasonal themes.

The merchandiser's job has to be to provide guidance to the buyer to procure within the budget parameters. In short it can be described as providing the buyer with a shopping list or range plan that allows them to go out and fill in the blanks on the plan while buying product. This activity requires the careful management of the "open to buy" which can often be a source of tension between the buyer who always tends to want more and the merchandiser who holds the purse strings. A good deal of emotional maturity and teamwork on both sides is therefore critical for a successful partnership.

Sadly the merchandising role is often branded as a dull, boring number crunching task in accordance with mathematical calculations and while it is this, it can be better described as a creative manipulation of numbers. This task is highly rewarding when positive trade results are achieved or alternatively equally as depressing when these do not materialise. The role can be likened to that of a husband who places his entire salary on a dead cert horse at the races which was by no means appreciated by his wife. However when the horse won he was similarly unpopular for not putting more money on the horse!

Like the buying role, the merchandiser deals with different activities simultaneously as part of the team across a number of seasons and therefore requires high levels of multi-tasking and re-prioritising in the forward planning, problem resolution, critical milestone management, analysis and timeous action implementation.

As the actual trade takes place the results need to be carefully analysed and immediate action plans initiated in order to maximise the opportunities and minimise the levels of markdowns that erode the profits. For these reasons they need to be logical, reliable, and consistent in order to take decisions based on fact.

The regular timeous generation of reports detailing sales analysis, stock levels and forward planning needs are distributed to all team members and to senior management. Often numeric information and commercial analysis is demanded on an immediate ad-hoc basis which adds pressure to the job function and can be very disruptive to routines which in such situations requires the merchandiser to adapt quickly and effectively.

The merchandiser plays an integral role during the presentation at product reviews from the numbers perspective which influences the agreed product mix and justification of the levels of sales budgets.

A detailed understanding is necessary of the stores and the customer profile inherent to respective stores that are best met through the attributes of the ranges in terms of styling, colour and size that are put on offer within the store space constraints. The task is best described by the saying "plan each store as if it is your own" which could never be truer.

With sophisticated IT development and the availability of various software packages, some of which may be developed exclusively for the retailer, will provide quick sales analysis, production planning and afford the ability to make sound decisions based on accurate data. This information is especially necessary to give guidance to the allocator or distributor who will be sending the appropriate quantities to satisfy the store's needs as well as give direction as to the level of repeat buys for products that are trading above expectations.

Some organisational structures do differentiate the allocation function between the merchandiser who focuses on the forecasting and production planning and that of the allocator or location planner who will be responsible to distribute the product to the stores in the most appropriate combinations of styles, colour and sizes that meet the store profiles. This function can be housed as an extension within the buying division or may be part of a separate centralised group where an allocator may be responsible for a diverse number of departments. The benefits of such a centralised structure is that there could be a cost saving advantage especially where smaller departments do not warrant a dedicated staff member but added to this is a pool of knowledge which develops a highly skilled team who are able to cross pollinate information, coordinate inter departmental promotions effectively and develop consistent techniques and skills. The identification of common emerging trends will contribute to the optimisation of sales and assist in the control of stock quantities at a very detailed level and thereby maximise profits. Close connections to the departmental merchandisers is maintained to ensure that their actions are aligned to the departmental strategy and plans.

The need for the diversification of the function also makes more sense from the point of view in that where the distribution function is retained within the department it inevitably adds to the increasing workload of the merchandiser. The departmental merchandiser task has more and more been impacted on by the development, the implementation and mastering of complex and sophisticated information systems that analyse sales and stock with added forward planning functionalities.

Many such systems are able to integrate with other supporting IT platforms such as supplier performance, technological measurement, critical path management, ordering, logistical and store systems. The added management of a complex allocation system that is necessary to move the stock to stores is more and more difficult with the result that the incumbent is in danger of being drawn into concentrating on and coping with the intricate detail. As a result, the merchandiser runs the risk of losing sight of the bigger objectives as set out in the strategy and operational plans and the consequent degrading of the inherent merchant intuition becomes very real.

The merchandiser needs to effectively manage and develop the merchandising team which can, not unlike the buying role, consist of an assistant merchandiser or trainee who aspire to be a merchandiser.

The role ensures cohesion of activities that have to be synchronized based on actual sales performance through the formalised interaction with other stakeholders such as the buyers and technologists. This contact is usually in the form of regular, typically weekly, departmental meetings where corrective decisions and plans of action are agreed. Frequent association with the points of sale in stores through written communications and reports as well as formal site visits are critical to keep aligned with the customer's preferences and emerging trends and confirm that the stores are sharing the same vision of the overall strategy.

The need to guide suppliers assertively in terms of prioritisation and the achievement of deadlines is critical to meet the suitable stock requirements at any point in time, particularly in relation to peak seasonal periods or key events. For example, once winter breaks, which it does every year except the exact date is not easy to predict, the objective is to have the right stocks in place such as knitwear, thermal underwear, scarves and the like in sufficient quantities to meet the rush. The usual manner to assist in the anticipation of the weather trend is done through reference to previous years data when the weather changes happened which also help to understand variations in out of ordinary performance at particular times. The challenge is therefore to have the appropriate quantities in the stores at the vital time while the maintenance of the balance of stocks must be adequate to cater for the demand without overstocking the stores ahead of planned stock targets. Events such as Easter, Christmas, Valentine's Day and Mother's day are easier to predict and the right levels of stock can be made more accurately available at the right time.

Where suppliers do not meet the required delivery dates, the merchandiser needs to manage the consequences that have to be applied for the underperformance. This can result in some very sensitive and emotional discussions and the negotiation of penalties typically in the form of discounts, sale or return agreements or even total cancellation which will no doubt impact negatively on both parties.

Technology

Technical Teams consist broadly of the fabric and garment technologists. Fabric technologists are highly trained specialists who focus on typically woven or knitted disciplines. Specialised products such as knitwear, tailoring and footwear require added knowledge of components and specific production machinery.

A major portion of the fabric technologist's task is the development and innovation of new fabrics and the enhancement of existing products. New fibres and blends of fibres such as the blending of natural and synthetic fibres, addition of chemicals to finishing process will possibly lead to new inventions and improvements such as better washability, softer handles, easy care properties like easy to iron, crease resistant finishes, rot resistant applications, seamless or seams that are glued that allow for smoother looks particularly for under garments, the evolvement of elastane products such as lycra which revolutionised active and casual wear and the enhancement of thermal properties of winter undergarments. The success of such developments which add to the profitability as well as the form and function necessitates a close working relationship with suppliers, mills and value adders.

Garment technology have the responsibility to ensure that the make-up of the garment meets the set down criteria and the componentry like buttons, interlinings and threads are of the standard that is functional and are not inferior.

Many factories have developed specified technological capabilities that have been built around the production of a particular category of garments relevant to them which vary from factory to factory or even within the same plant. The garment technologist must understand this implicitly and exploit this knowledge to its fullest.

The relationship with the commercial team is sometimes strained as the ideal level of form and function can be challenged by the need to market the product at the most commercially competitive price.

The objective of the garment technologist is to ensure that quality is not compromised. The tasks essential to achieve this can be varied, for example, the assessment of potential manufacturers and fabric mills to ensure that the established standards are achievable, the specification of raw materials, overseeing sampling stages and ensuring that any delays which may result through the process do not compromise the delivery prerequisites.

In safeguarding that the all quality standards are met particularly through the inspection of garments, inspectors need to possess specific skills. Quality controllers should be ethical, sincere and honest, open mindedly being willing to consider alternatives, be diplomatic and tactful in their dealings with people and are able to actively observe their surroundings as well as perceive and adapt to varying situations.

The technologist has an intimate knowledge of the supplier base through historical awareness as well as from continually researching new and existing suppliers. As the sourcing specialist they have to guide buying teams in the selection of the most appropriate manufacturer for the various types of product. It is also very essential that they are conscious of the fabric prominence for the forthcoming season as dictated by the strategies and budget levels to ensure that there is sufficient capacities at the relevant mills to meet the overall demands without compromising quality.

The task of assessing potentially new suppliers is a role that may be included in the stable of the technical team or it may be hived off to defined sourcing specialists who are knowledgeable team members that recognise the strengths and weaknesses of suppliers and based on this where best to place orders accordingly.

Suppliers are assessed on various criteria such as their management infrastructure, financial stability, specialised equipment availability, fabric specialty, levels of innovation, fashion or basic production orientation, the other retailers they serve, their flexibility of cost negotiability and social responsibility policies. Other external factors that may well influence the selection of suppliers could be those like prevailing exchange rates, remuneration policies and physical locality.

In summary, the significance must be emphasised that the diverse buying teams all have to have a clear informed understanding of each other's roles and priorities and that they are aligned to ensure all their tasks are integrated to achieve the goal of delivering consistent quality products manufactured by appropriately skilled suppliers on time all the time. This is especially imperative in the case of more complex products such as corsetry, tailored garments and knitwear.

The handling, packaging, storage and movement of the product through the supply channels has to be done in such a way that the quality of the product is not allowed to deteriorate in any way whatsoever. As some product is sourced from more distant locations a newer trend is to contract the technical function out to approved independent technical service providers or to trusted garment and fabric suppliers themselves who understand and are committed to the standards required. These service providers are thereby able to approve samples, perform quality control and be responsible for the eventual release of the finished product.

THE SELLING OPTIONS
There are many ways to expose the product to the customer in the hope that they will take a positive decision during the shopping process. More often than not, the nature of the product will influence the type of channel that is selected but whatever format that the retail store takes, it remains very simply a part of the integrated supply chain whereby goods are purchased in large quantities directly from a manufacturer, wholesaler, trading house or agent to be sold on in smaller quantities to the end user.

Retailing can be done in the more traditional fixed locations like stores or markets but in recent years there has been the evolvement of more innovative ways of selling the product, a typical example being "pop up" shops whereby a temporary location is used in a busy environment which is possibly a sports event, trade show or similar location where large volumes of potential customers are present. It is also an easy way of promoting goods or the carrying out of special launches.

In the modern era of technology the internet is probably the fastest growing medium through which to sell product. Online websites now exist for all types of goods and all the major traders as well as dedicated online retailers are spending large amounts of money to set up their sites in such a way that they are very user friendly, faster and most attractive with secure, easy payment methods.

The main objectives of such sites is to enable the offer of products, create a level of trust and inspire the customer to make a purchase. The establishment of trust can be aided by the use of testimonials whereby the experience of past customers affirm the selling proposition.

Door to door deliveries at an additional fee or which alternatively may be absorbed by the retailer are carried out by sophisticated courier services from various highly efficient distribution centres. International purchases in foreign currencies are also relatively easy to do in this way and customers receive the parcels within a reasonable period of time.

Another option is that the retailer may choose to carry out picking of stock from brick and mortar stores which are in close proximity to the online customer but it should be noted that this choice does bring challenges in sustaining consistent full availabilities and maintaining accurate data integrity. Similarly, some retailers offer the facility of "click and collect" whereby the customer places an order on line and at a time convenient to them collects the order from a designated store. There are also out sourced specialised delivery services that can deliver to varied pick up points across a number of facilities which in fact could be another retailer in an area which is not related to the original source of the purchase which allows for greater ease of convenience that suits the lifestyle of the customer.

The problem that customers do have is that they are not able to try on the garments so retailers need to devise some convenient special service options such as the provision of critical body measurements to assist in the determination of an appropriate size.

The fact however remains that there are many on line shopping platforms popping up every day but the challenge remains for them remains for all of them is to convert visitors to actual buyers. In order that this is achieved effectively there must be certain fundamentals present. The landing page must be compelling consisting of great visual images and bold statements that highlight the features of the products on offer. The presentation of user reviews inspires confidence in the minds of potential buyers. The personalisation of customer accounts that based on their track record of previous purchases suggest new products that would be suited to their personal profile. What is of paramount importance is the constant striving for excellence through the products that are sold, the experience on the site, as well as the maintenance of great after sales and service.

Marketing teams utilise various types of techniques to effectively expose the product in the most attractive way to the market. Traditional channels in the form of print, radio, television, in house magazines, flyers, and point of sale material as well as the use of innovative medium such as in store digital signage as a tool when they are making purchasing decisions, permeating fragrances and suitable background music or a store branded radio station all attempt to enhance the shopping experience. The use of posters and bill boards, scratch cards and the like are still very prominent in varying formats, however in increasing magnitudes, the creative use of the electronic channels by way of websites, sms, e-mail and social media such as facebook and twitter are now very evident.

The three most popular social media platforms that are utilised to promote the business is Twitter, Facebook and Instagram. Briefly, Twitter allows the targeting the advertising according to interest categories, hashtags, promoted accounts, promoted tweets and promoted trends which allow the business to build followers through greater exposure, building brand awareness, sharing content and offering special deals.

Facebook which has a global membership of 1.5 billion is the largest platform in the world and therefore is like to provide the greatest exposure to the business. Adverts can be specifically directed to specific locations, genders, interests, workplaces, status and relationship statuses. Facebook remains a very cost effective means of advertising and if the message is accurate it can be extremely successful and effective.

Instagram is the fastest growing platform and it is estimated that at more than 45% of major brands use this platform to promote their goods. The advertisements can be done in the form of 15 second videos, and photo link advertisements. Typically Instagram is more suited to brand niche advertising and social media managers need not to tale this forum too seriously but rather see it as a way to have a bit of fun and actively interact with their community. In this way it can be seen as a tool to build long lasting relationships with the audience and the brand.

It should be noted that today's customers hop from researching products on their smartphones to viewing them physically in a brick and mortar store or ordering them online without hesitation. While this has transformed the retail experience compared to a few years ago the merchant's priorities of driving sales, enhancing efficiency and delivering the absolute service have still remained the same.

Up until recently the choice of medium was simply based on the sheer traffic volumes that were enjoyed. Fortunately the approach has changed significantly and the determining factors which influence the decision of what platform to apply is now more customer centralised in that marketing campaigns use those platforms which their target customers frequent the most. In other words the company realises that the customer data is linked to the people rather than the devices and thereby can create personal experiences across varying channels.

The systematic collection of customer data through the interactive media allows the customer profiles to be analysed and targeted in a more scientific way. Loyalty programmes are very popular and mostly reward the customer either in the form of points which can be cashed in at a later stage for the purchase or provide an immediate discount at the till point. Such programmes are not only extremely effective in significantly improving sales and profits but they also allow the retailer to interpret in detail the buying habits of the customer and consequently thereby are able to better service the consumer needs. Other benefits include providing the retailer's reputation a boost and improve on-line presence and drives additional traffic to the site and thereby gain more customers.

While shopping generally refers to the activity of simply buying a product it has become very much a recreational activity whereby a visit to the shopping mall becomes a wonderful experience which may or may not necessarily result in any purchase being made. Some malls may have added attractions such as theatres, ice skating rinks, stages for entertainment and even larger magnetisms such as aquariums and fun parks while facilities such as gyms are not an uncommon appendage. Restaurant and fast food eateries are an integral part which are often positioned in centrally located food halls where both the major brands and specialised restaurants are represented.

The dominant tenants are the major retailers who are regarded to be the crowd pullers. The main mix comprise of large food chains together with typical mass clothing retailers while other stores such as general chains provide the bulk of hard and specialist goods like electronics, appliances, stationery, furnishings, jewelry, pharmaceuticals and sports shops.

A complex combination of line shops who derive their name due to the fact that they flank the interlinking walkways between the major tenants and tend to be more exclusive in their offerings. The rentals are usually at a much higher rate and the closest adjacency to a major tenant comes at a premium. Line shops will typically include outlets such as hairdressers, opticians, beauticians, boutiques, dedicated outdoor gear retailers, accessory specialists, luggage shops, photographic stores, religious retailers selling inspirational product and even tattoo parlours. Other options include the barrow type outlets selling product such as ties and accessories and specialized delicacies.

What is also evolving to a greater degree is the presence of international chains and brands from all over the world as it has become increasingly easy for stores to open due to improved technologies and exposure both from an IT perspective as well as the use of efficient transport methodologies. It has reached a stage where very few major retailers ignore opportunities to trade internationally especially where domestic markets have become saturated and increasingly competitive. The lure of new emerging markets are great but can be challenging in terms of the differing profiles of customers and culture considerations as well as the unforeseen detection of hidden costs.

Malls are strategically positioned close to residential dense areas and the science of the mix of line shops supported by the major tenants are largely influenced by the demographics of the area that they serve. Such malls may be supported by adjacent discount shopping centres which mostly include many clothing, shoe and factory outlet stores. Factory shops enable manufacturers or traders to market over runs, rejects, problem lines at reduced prices in locations that enjoy lower rentals. Liquor outlets, hardware stores and nurseries are also frequently seen adjacent to the main shopping complex.

A factor that should be addressed in the layout of malls is the ease of shopping and the implementation of plans for the free flow of traffic which does not stress the customers particularly during peak times when the mall corridors are jam packed with people. This state of affairs is leading to an ever increasing trend towards convenience shopping where the establishment of smaller shopping centres on the fringes of suburbs dispenses with the anxiety and lessens the time required to complete the shop.

The mall has largely been the cause of the demise of the "high street" store as is evident by the many major chain stores who have succumbed. The operations have consequently closed or have relocated to the shopping centres outside the city. However, there is still a place in certain instances for these stores to remain as is seen in some cities where there is in fact a reverse trend as there is still a density of office workers as well a growing inclination to live within the city centre which has led to surplus office space being transformed into apartment blocks or new developments being constructed.

Traditional general stores and co-operatives offering a broad range of everything for the community and mom and pop family run shops who purchased from the travelling salesman most commonly found in the rural areas are now very far and few between. Centralised shopping locations consist most commonly of tenants where all the relevant chains being represented with the influx of the discount shops specialising in goods from the East, (some of which may have originated from dubious sources), are now in almost every town. This has sadly relegated these old fashioned stores to no longer being in existence.

Franchise stores offer the opportunity for individual traders to invest in a mass retail group and enjoy the benefit of the support from the chain's branding, quality products and marketing strategies. The advantage for the franchisee is that the expansion and market penetration can be accelerated with external investment and they enjoy a commission for goods sold without the risk of stock holding costs, overheads and staffing expenses. The success of a franchise venture will depend mostly on enough working capital, reliable support from the franchisor and the emotional involvement in the business of the franchisee with suitable staff in the right location at affordable rentals.

In days gone by the goods were stored in walk-in counters often being displayed behind glass and in drawers with sales assistants serving the customer from within the unit as well as manning a till stationed at each counter. While this way of serving customers was very effective from an interaction point of view it soon became unsustainable due to the demands of mass retailing and convenience for the customer.

The newer formats of stores are well lit, uncluttered and appealing to the customer. They house easy to access product which is in sufficient quantities with well demarcated information through attractive signage. Displays whether on shelves, tables or garment rails are well thought out and coordinated in cameo presentations that are lit in such a way that suggest to the customer how the product pieces can be worn together in terms of lifestyle and colouration. Displays are adjacent to complementary customer needs, for example women's skirts will be located close to the blouse displays which will be adjacent to the ladies trousers. The ladies outerwear will most likely be next to the lingerie department which will lead into ladies sleepwear. There can also be a thread of the chosen similar colour themes throughout which are being promoted at that point in time.

in highly visible areas such as aisles, window displays or walls which change regularly to convey the message of prevailing stories in order to attract and engage the customer. Seasonal changes, special events, promotional activity and colour themes are typically introduced in this way and thereby sustain the impact of newness, freshness and excitement. The customer not only has a pleasant experience considering the proposition but the potential opportunity of a sale is maximised.

Pay points and change rooms are conveniently placed and the design of these units are such that they lessen the frustration that comes with the inevitable waiting periods.

Personal interaction with the customer by any staff member whether they are the sales assistants or management can never be substituted. Service remains of paramount importance in ensuring that they can illustrate to the customer the ways in which styles and colours of the different components can tastefully be worn together.

Payment methodologies are also focused on in order to ensure that the customer has an enjoyable experience and is not frustrated by the task of having to stand in long queues. Technologies are advancing at a rapid pace to minimise long queues and newer examples are in the form of a shopping basket being scanned in total which eliminates the individual handling of each product, the evolvement of the contactless card which does not require the customer having to swipe cards, provide pin numbers or sign any slips. All that is required is the simple tapping of the card against a card reader for payment to be processed. Another innovative process is the establishment of self-service pay points where by the customer checks out their own goods and thereby saves considerable time. Whatever the sophistication of the payment methodologies there is one basic requirement that retailers need to make provision for and that is having a card facility. Without such a facility they will not survive for the following simple reasons. Cards are now a global form of payment and are particularly important to international travellers. They are convenient for everyone as they minimise the necessity to carry cash and are therefore less of a security risk and should the card get lost or stolen the can be quickly cancelled via a telephone call which in itself makes them safer than carrying cash.. Card payment also enables bigger purchases, which may or may not be a good thing but research shows that customers tend to make about thirty percent bigger purchases as opposed to only using cash. Because a card leaves a trace it allows for accurate tracking of transaction history and enables more responsible management of financial resources.

For the retailer, the advantages of card facilities is that they enable real time transactions which includes reporting and reconciliation. Added to this they empower the acceleration of transactions, tighten control and security and most importantly reduce costs across the board.

The unfortunate downside is that they are a soft target for cyber criminals and therefore need to be carefully protected through disciplined usage and password or pin code control.

The need for refurbishment and revitalisation of stores and displays is an ongoing process, which although being costly, regularly presents the customer with a fresh and exciting environment to enjoy the shopping experience and avoid being faced with stale, run down and drab looking stores that undermine even the most attractive merchandise.

As with the buying teams, the selling teams also consist of a mix of skills that are coordinated in such a way that the customer has a most satisfying shopping experience.

The team is spearheaded by general manager who is the head of the store. This position maybe supported by an assistant officer and they will ensure that the overall co-ordination of all the roles will deliver the most efficient running of the operation. A classic structure that they will manage consists of commercial or departmental managers each of whom will be responsible for a segment of the store.

Their role will focus on ensuring that the displays are constantly fully stocked and that they are optimally positioned and displayed proportionately appropriate to the customer demand. By way of illustration the most popular product will normally be in the front of the racks and displayed at the eye level of the customer. The size of the display will be proportionate to the relative demand, in other words, in the ideal world a product that represents twenty percent of the sales will enjoy twenty percent of the space of the relevant display area. Exceptions to this principle may occur where the product may be bulky and will have to be pallet stacked on the floor. An example of this would be nappies, duvets and cushions.

A basic layout format of the various groups and departments and product which will accommodate the flow of the customer in such a way that the greatest exposure is provided. A typical layout is reflected below.

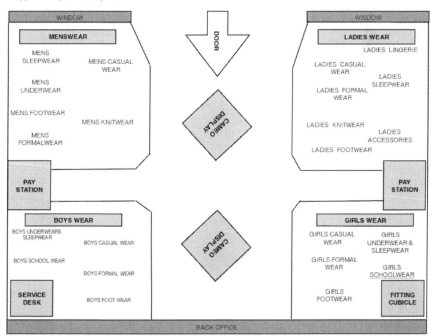

The challenge is to ensure that there is the optimum number of well trained, knowledgeable and positive staff that can best serve the customers without the overhead costs being put under pressure. The service disposition should apply for the entire shopping experience from the time that the customer is greeted at the front door until the transaction is finalised at the till point and the customer leaves the store with the added objective being that the customer will always look forward to returning to the store. Even where a sale may not transpire the offering of advice or patiently helping consider alternatives is part and parcel of ensuring that the customer will return.

Selling teams are supported by other staff functions such as the human resource officer who will be responsible for the personnel functions as well as the shift scheduling of staff. This task is imperative to ensure optimum staffing which is appropriate for the inconstant number of customers over the various times during the day, week month and year of trade. A flexible, part time work force is required which can be more than two thirds of the total store staff and because some of the hours of work are unsocial such as weekend or after normal hours variable rates of remuneration or extra time off will apply.

PROCESS FLOW OF KEY RETAIL ACTIVITIES
While a lot of activities are required from conceptualisation to the eventual offering of a completed product to the customer they do nevertheless follow a relative set sequence of events even though there may be at any point in time where they can possibly overlap each other.

The journey commences broadly with strategy formulation and the strategic planning for each stakeholder area, the creation of a merchandise plan through to the buying of the product within the budgetary parameters. The commercial team have the support of the technology teams to establish the technical requirements as well as the sourcing of appropriate suppliers in order to enable the production of the product.

The packaging is detailed to assist in the marketing of the product and protect the garments in transit and storage. Orders are initiated and the critical production milestones are managed in such a way to ensure delivery deadlines are met timeously.

During production the quality inspection and supplier performance management takes place and once the order is complete the products will be allocated and delivered either directly to stores or to a storage facility. In some instances there may be value added processes applied to the goods after which they will be transported to stores.

Once the goods are on offer to the customer the sales are analysed and reviewed in order to make adjustments where necessary. At the end of the season the lessons learnt are noted and applied to the strategy development for the new season.

PACKAGING TECHNOLOGY
The packaging of a product is largely the responsibility of a packaging technologist and plays a critical role in the presentation, protection and communication of information to the consumer as well as taking into account the ecological demands of the environment.

The common purpose of packaging is that it physically protects the product against mechanical shocks, vibrations, varying temperatures, humidity and excessive handling during transit or warehousing. The usual provision of information whether it is on the packaging itself or through the use of labels, indicate any regulations that may apply, the usage and safety instructions, transport guidelines and lists the components and chemicals that were used in the production process.

Packaging assists in the sale of the product in that it serves as a "silent salesman". There is a communication of information through clever graphic design that encompasses the properties of the product, instructions as how to use the merchandise and the provision of safety warnings. Convenience is added by way of easy storage configurations, display conformity and the accommodation of barcoding information which is easily accessible for scanners to capture sales and stock keeping records and store them on a common data base.

Specialised packaging plays an important part in securing the product through the use of tamper proof mechanisms and can also be engineered to reduce the pilferage.

Over packaging should be avoided and where possible the utilisation of recycled or recyclable materials in the manufacturing process is encouraged without affecting the functional properties.

Outer cartons must adhere to weight and dimension stipulations and should be able to be easily handled on warehouse equipment such as conveyer belts, pallets and storage slots.

Of the two types, primary packaging enjoys the journey of the product right to the end user while secondary packaging is that which is discarded at various points during the journey.

Examples of primary packaging are self- adhesive tickets which carry the barcode detail, price, reference numbers, colour and size as well as date codes. Swing tickets are used where adhesive tickets are not appropriate and may also be independently attached in order to highlight any unique features of the product. Invariably adhesive tickets are applied to presentation packs, wallets and plastic bags.

Sew in labels are typically a satin tape which is sewn into the garment side or neck seam and carry wash care instructions, product reference numbers, size information, fabric composition, country of origin as well as safety instructions. The fibre content must be described by its generic name but may be accompanied by a brand name or a trade mark. An example would be where woollen products will display the wool mark for which the supplier will have qualified to utilise through their manufacturing process.

An example of garment care and reference label

EXAMPLE OF A GARMENT CARE AND REFERENCE LABEL

Care markings are not legally required but are commonly indicated by the universal symbols that are consistent and accurate, for example, where a garment needs to be hand washed only and not machine washed it will be highlighted using the relevant symbol

Universal care instruction symbols are key to the garment label and the most common are outlined below

Symbol	Description	Symbol	Description
〈60°〉	WASHING WATER TEMPERATURE	⊠	DO NOT TUMBLE DRY
🖐	HAND WASH ONLY	▨	DRIP DRY IN SHADE
⊔	WASH ON SENSITIVE PROGRAMMES	▤	DRIP DRY
⊠	DO NOT WASH	⊟	DRY FLAT
Ⓟ	DRY CLEANABLE	⊓	DRY ON HANGER
⊗	DO NOT DRY CLEAN	⊠	DO NOT IRON
⊠	DO NOT USE BLEACH	🜕	IRON WITH WARM IRON
⊠	DO NOT TUMBLE DRY	🜕	IRON WITH HOT IRON

Country of origin is displayed on labels to indicate geographically where the significant stage of production took place. In most countries this is a legal requirement even if the garment may have some components that originate from other parts of the world. Apart from it being law, the identification gives the consumer the choice of which countries that they may wish to support or not support for political or emotional reasons and participate in buy local promotional campaigns that are designed to stimulate local employment.

Swing tags that describe features or unique properties of products have to be truthful in terms of fit for purpose and of the quality standard that is expected by the customer. Where the product does not meet these claims they can be deemed to be misleading and could have legal implications that can be enforced either by the user or competitors who may feel unfairly disadvantaged. An example of this could be that where a ticket describes the garment as being non-iron but after a few washes it has to be ironed.

Secondary packaging are items such as outer cartons, over bags for hanging product, hanger size indicators, stock room and store address labels, the outer carton product detail and supplier detail stamps.

The procuring and specifying of ecologically friendly packaging should always be done keeping the safety of the environs top of mind. Printing should be done keeping volatile compound emissions to a minimum through, for example, the use of vegetable based ink that are free from heavy metals.

Measures need to be put in place to keep waste of inks, ink tins, and paper to a minimum and the cleaning and recirculation of polluted water should be promoted. Paper packaging and corrugated cartons ought to contain a percentage of recycled papers and must not to have been bleached using chlorine. Plastic packaging should be of recyclable materials such as polypropylene and polyethylene.

Packaging costs will also vary for different types of product. The size of the cartons required to transport the product is determined by the dimensions of height and width that must protect and accommodate the garment comfortably. The in store presentation requirements will also affect the overall cost from the point of view that allowance may be needed for hangers as well as additional swing tickets.

Where goods are imported, duties need to be taken into consideration. Duties are normally determined against the free on board value or in other words the cost to place it on the deck of the ship. They can also be calculated as ex works which is the cost as at the completion of production.

Exchange rates are a critical factor. The option to purchase currency ahead of time at a fixed rate to finance the cost provides the peace of mind that the costs will be stable even if the day to day rates fluctuate. If currency is not bought ahead but goods are purchased at the prevailing rates the retailer may be forced to revise selling prices to ensure the achievement of the target margin.

Different categories of products attract different tariff duties at the receiving country depending on country of origin and manufacture as well as protection policies of local production.

The cost to transport the goods from the place of manufacture will vary for local goods or from the port by the clearing agent, depending on the location of the retailer in relation to the supplier or port, the size of the cartons or container and the mode of transport. Included in this section would be freight and warehousing charges.

The typical elements of a product costing and examples of approximate proportions will be

ELEMENT	DEPENDENCY	CATEGORY
TRANSPORT 5%	Different methods of transport used.	Transport / landing 20%
DUTY 30 - 40%	Taxes levied against the import of goods as specified by the local government.	
SUPPLIER MARGIN 10%	Supplier margin can vary between 5% and 15%.	
WASH AND TRIMS 5%	Costs allocated to special processes or trims.	
PACKAGING 7%	Total cost of all packaging, including presentation.	Production costs 80%
LABOUR 28%	The standard minute rates will differ from country to country, depending on operational complexity.	
FABRIC AND MATERIAL 50%	Will be influenced by the garment rating, which will dictate how much fabric is used to manufacture the garment.	

In addition to the product costs as outlined above there are other costs that need to be taken into account in order to get product to market. These can be categorised basically into two categories, firstly being additional costs to the supplier such as the base overhead costs being the total for rent, electricity, administration costs and the like that will always be there and which must be apportioned per product unit.

The second category can be described as being unrelated to the product directly that have to be paid. The main type of such costs are settlement discount agreements, marketing contributions, finance costs and royalties. These together with the product costs will deliver the final cost of the garment.

Points to note in the review of costs are in cases where the supplier throws in vague and unsubstantiated reasons to justify increases. It is essential that the retailer tests such requests to ensure they carry merit.

A typical instance is where the statement is made that wages have gone up and a new costing is proposed. A cross check is required to determine the proportion of what labour represents of the total costing. In the above example this would be the 28% for labour and apply the increase to this part and reconcile to the proposal.

Where increases are attributed to material increases an effort should be made to investigate the trend in the industry and do some comparisons even if they may be a bit crude. If your research shows that the increase is not in line with the trend, the supplier should be encouraged to find a better source and not to pass on the cost of their inefficiencies.

The use of exchange rate fluctuations to motivate cost price changes is more easily resolved as the average movement can be tracked over a period of time and applied. It is a possibility that in fact there might have been an improvement. Foreign currency could also have an influence depending at what price the supplier or retailer may have covered forward.

If the retailer's volumes are increasing significantly the opportunity exists to negotiate a discount in cost price to share the benefits of the improved scale of efficiencies. A point to note is that while this practice is not discouraged, the smaller retailer may not be able to finance the larger volumes of product or growth based incentives. Even with the benefit of a greater margin, the viability remains to be dependent on the organic growth of the chain, for example, the addition of new stores in order to accommodate the higher buying volumes.

A costing approach which is often employed by retailers is that of requesting appropriate suppliers to tender for a product. In order that this is done fairly and equitably the exact same specifications need to be provided to the potential suppliers. Cross costing comparison between suppliers is a popular option where there are large programmes up for grabs and is unlikely to be used for once off high fashion inputs.

For a retailer to commit to high volume programmes, it is a key requisite that the potential suppliers fulfil some basic requirements in that they must be financially stable, have a reliable track record in terms of delivery performance, provide consistent quality with up to date compliancy audits and will be able to cope with the required volumes which could include the agreement to hold a minimum stock holding. The supplier should also be flexible enough to be able to make styling changes to the product where necessary.

The key stipulations for use with cross costing or tenders which will be provided is a detailed style sheet, comprehensive specifications of fabric and trims, the garment measurements with the range of sizes, volumes, a target cost price, packaging requirements and packing methods, delivery dates or production flow.

ORDERING

After the negotiations are completed and the decision to award the production of a style to the supplier is taken, an order has to be drafted to reflect the commitment to the supplier.

The signed order for the supplier is created and placed by the retailer for the entire season in the case of a continuity product or possibly monthly for input styles. It is imperative that it must be done timeously to ensure the required completion date is realistically achievable and the production lead time required will be determined by careful critical path production management.

While the order is in essence a contractual document it will be subject to the overall terms and conditions that are entered into in a memorandum of agreement that is drawn up separately when a manufacturer is appointed as a certified supplier. Production can only commence once the final approved order is in the possession of the supplier.

The contract or the order is the document that details the terms by which the retailer takes ownership of the goods in exchange or payment of an agreed price.

The timing of orders is done according to the range plan guidelines and each supplier will be provided with an extract specific to them for the season. This production programme will indicate the style details, quantities, size ratios and colour specifications which will enable them to plan the production capacity and will be used as the point of reference during follow up production progress meetings. Each style will also have a corresponding style specification sheet which confirm the costs, pack quantities, labels and tickets, wash and care details, testing requirements and the fabric as well as component information.

Orders may be amended where required. These adjustments are normally for quantities, dates, prices and size ratios. The changes need to be recorded on the contract and refer to the date of the alteration as well as the nature of the change.

It is advisable that any style changes require the order to be cancelled and be replaced by a new order as in essence it is a different product.

The order can have two status phases where a pre-production contract enables the supplier to procure fabrics, components, labelling and packaging and make a pre-production or pre shipment sample which will be submitted to the retailer for approval. The sample will serve as the set standard of quality that will be referred to should any disputes evolve in production or in stores.

Production may only commence once a final approved order is received by the supplier.

Documented programmes of continuity lines for the full season may serve as an authorised arrangement from which the supplier will be able to order the raw materials and components but they will only be able to commence production of agreed quantities, for example, for six weekly time periods upon the receipt of an approved contract. This gives the retailer the flexibility to make adjustments based on current performance. Such amendments may take the form of changes to quantities, size ratios and colour quantities.

Dependent on whether the supplier is local or offshore the delivery requirements need to be clearly outlined with all relevant contact details, delivery stipulations, carton markings and delivery addresses.

In the case of a local supplier, delivery is normally to a designated warehouse at an approved time. Off shore suppliers may have to deliver to an offshore centralised consolidation centre where the goods will be amalgamated by shipping agents into containers prior to shipping. Payment will be made in the foreign currency and will be dictated by the international commercial (INCO) terms applied.

Common INCO terms for the payment of imported goods will be FOB (Sea Freight) which is where payment is prior to shipment by sea either by bank wire or a letter of credit. The purchaser's bank releases payment upon receipt of certain documentation such as the bill of lading, packing lists or commercial invoice and is due when the goods are loaded on the ship and ownership is then transferred to the retailer. If the INCO term is FCA it carries the same conditions as FOB except that the transportation is by air.

CFR (Sea and Air Freight) describes the situation where the supplier is responsible for the costs of transport to the destination port. While ownership only transfers when the goods reach the destination, the retailer is responsible for the goods while they are in transit and therefore they would have to take out insurance for this period. If the supplier does this then the INCO term applied is CIF (cost, insurance, freight).

Added to the costs are government duties which can be applied in the form of a percentage dependent on the various customs categories that the product falls into.

In terms of air freight it should be noted that the cost is often prohibitive as it is dictated by volume and weight and therefore is usually only applied to small and high value items or where an urgent stock need is required in order to meet a launch date.

When placing orders for imports it is critical to take into account the lead times that need to be added on to ensure the required delivery and launch dates are met. Lead time can be described loosely as the time that it takes for product to be delivered from the factory to the back door of the retailer's warehouse or distribution centre. This becomes increasingly complex when the factory is off shore as there are a whole host of additional activities that have to take place before the retailer eventually receives the goods.

Pre shipment activities may involve the delivery to an off shore consolidation centre where different orders may be combined to make the full use of a container cost effective. Part deliveries in different containers can also make the consolidation and sequence of packing more complicated where there are different orders possibly also for different retailers.

In terms of the pre shipment critical path that needs to be adhered to prior to shipment is triggered by the supplier's confirmation that this will be met about three weeks before the ship date and approximately a week later the forwarder will advise the vessel and booking details at which time the supplier will send the pre shipment sample to the retailer with quality audit reports to request approval to ship.

A typical order for imported and local products will probably be as follows

ORDER									
RETAILER XYZ									

ORDER NO.		DATE				
SUPPLIER		ORDER STATUS	Pre production	Production		
SUPPLIER REFERENCE		COMPLETE/SHIP DATE				
PAYMENT TERMS		LAUNCH DATE				
DELIVERY METHOD		PACK QUANTITY				
DELIVER TO		TOTAL QUANTITY				
		COST VALUE				
		SELLING VALUE				

SKU NUMBER	STYLE NUMBER	STYLE DESCRIPTION	COLOUR	TOTAL COLOUR UNITS	SIZE	TOTAL SIZE UNITS	COST PRICE	SELLING PRICE
100023564	12345	Basic t-shirt	White	1000	S	200	45,00	99,99
100023565					M	400	45,00	99,99
100023566					L	300	50,00	110,00
100023567					XL	100	50,00	110,00
100023568	12345	Basic t-shirt	Black	2000	S	400	45,00	99,99
100023569					M	800	45,00	99,99
100023570					L	600	50,00	110,00
100023571					XL	200	50,00	110,00

BUYER SIGN		MANAGEMENT SIGN			
MERCHANDISER SIGN		SUPPLIER SIGN		DATE	

The information typically included on the order is as follows and will be stored on a data base system for any interested party that needs to access the detail.

Supplier reference number and name

Order number

Date that order was raised

Port of loading

Shipment date and launch dates

Shipping method

Method of payment

Payment terms

Point of delivery

Style number

Style description

Colour break down and quantity

Labelling instructions

Special terms or conditions of trade

SKU number

Size breakdown

Quantities

Cost Price less any negotiated discounts

Selling Price

Number of cartons

Carton dimensions

Number of units per inner pack

Number of inner packs per outer carton

Signatures of authorization to buy are most commonly those of the buyer, merchandiser and a member of senior management. The omission of any of the signatures could result in the order being rendered invalid in the case of a disagreement. A supplier signature is often the rule but the acceptance of the order is in essence the recognition of all the terms and conditions of the order.

It is not uncommon for planning production schedules or provisional orders to be handed over to the supplier prior to the issuing of an official order, particularly in the case of replenishment product where the supplier needs to plan capacity requirements, order raw materials and components but this is by no means the go ahead to commence production. Without the completed signed order no knife may be put to the fabric.

The higher level order may be supplemented by a detailed specification pack and a critical path management document that serves as an appendage to the order and reflect the details and quality references of the fabric and components, sample submission requirements, technical tests, labelling instructions, packaging reference numbers and specifications.

The buying and merchandising team will use the basic information to interrogate orders at any time to check, monitor and if required will amend the orders which may be, for example, quantity or date related. Other areas of operation or parties will also need to have access to orders in order that their activities are completed timeously to safeguard that the final completion date is met.

Technology has to utilise the detail to ensure in the process of managing the critical path that all tests, quality control during the manufacturing process, garment fittings and rail samples are completed timeously.

The finance department need to know all the costing details and terms of payment as well as the proposed selling price to ensure that there is sufficient cash flow available to enable payment and be able to monitor the achievement of the gross profit margins.

The IT departments need to be aware of all orders for the provision of the SKU numbers as well as cater for the generation of the swing tickets or labels that are attached to the garments indicating the style number, colour, size and price detail which are either sent to the suppliers in bulk or the data files are transmitted to those suppliers that have the facilities to generate their own SKU tickets.

The distribution centre must have sight of the orders in the pipeline to assess the size of proposed deliveries going forward to ensure that they are in a position to plan sufficient resources in terms of staffing, equipment, space capacity and that sufficient transport is booked to deliver the goods speedily to stores.

The space capacity requirements both in the warehouse and stores will depend largely on the packing configurations in terms of the storage outer carton which is how the goods will be stored, allocated and transported to stores and the inner packs which are otherwise known as the saleable unit that will be presented to the potential consumer.

Examples of packing configuration below where selling units of t-shirts is singles and are packed ten in an outer carton and where socks selling units is in a three pack and there are ten three packs in the outer carton

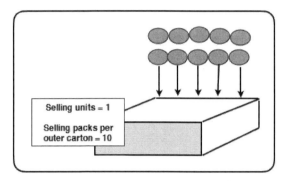

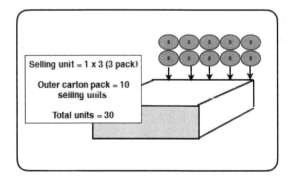

PRODUCT ALLOCATION

Once production is complete the supplier will advise via a report what volumes by size and colour are complete and packaged ready for dispatch to the addresses as stipulated by the retailer.

In a perfect world the intake will match the volumes as indicated on the intake line in the original plan as highlighted earlier. However, sales will never be exactly as expected as the customers do not have prior knowledge of the plans and will always buy differently. Coupled to this the amount of over or under production due to a reject factor could result in availabilities being higher or lower than what the supplier was meant to make and therefore the actual closing stock at the end of each period will definitely vary to the expectation. Markdown values are also continually different to that planned.

Stocks and sales are the anchor targets that are consistently aimed for with the intake being the balancing variable to bring the plan back in line. In the hypothetical exercise below done for Month 1 of the plan it is illustrated as to how the intake is manipulated over the four weeks of the month in order to meet the original stock targets.

It must be noted that the monetary intake requirement needs to be converted to units at the style/colour level to enable the stock availability to be allocated and distributed.

The allocation of product from the availability reports provided by suppliers or stocks stored in the warehouse takes on two methodologies. The input type products, usually for seasonal launches or fashion styles are described as "push" products while the continuity product which is replenished in empathy to sales performance are known as "pull" products where allocations are triggered by minimum stock level points and stopped by the maximum stock level thresholds.

The key differentiators of these types of products are that "push" styles cater for peak sales before being replaced. These styles attract a higher markdown volume as they are removed off display once the range becomes broken as they need to make way for the new themes that the replacement input styles bring.

"Pull" styles determine the requirements based on replacement of actual sales to a pre-determined build to level of stock. The calculation of the quantity of stock required will be the be determined by the amount of intake needed to meet the stock target that is either dynamically determined by the set weeks sales forward cover or is maintained at a static level over time.

"Pull" styles should typically be continuity items that have a predictable rate of sale and have a balanced availability of sufficient volumes of stock from the lowest level to meet the fluctuating demand. The supplier's production planning therefore has to be consistently reliable and flexible to sustain this condition.

The "pull" principle can be illustrated as follows

STOCK
LEVEL

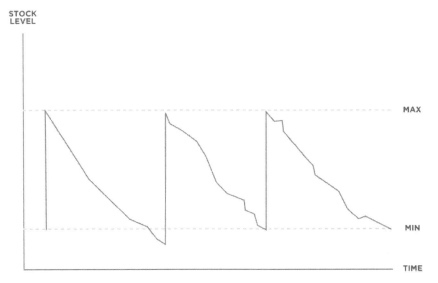

The automatic replenishment or distribution of products is often performed through the use of sophisticated technical allocation systems and are most suitable for the basic continuity product that have consistent predictable sales patterns and for store displays which are laid out according to a centralised space planning system.

The application needs to be merged with the historical sales data and the planned overall sales going forward. In order to achieve a constant replenishment over time a technique of smoothing is utilised where a weighting factor is applied to sales which deviate from the norm due to an unusual event and in such cases the system will use the adjusted realistic level of sale in the algorithm to derive the most appropriate forward allocations.

In the case where there is a launch of new lines, the new line can be linked to the pattern of a similar current style. The performance of the new styles must therefore be very carefully monitored early on and adjusted if need be to ensure the best size provision as possible.

The manual overriding of calculated allocations at store level should only take place in exceptional circumstances for specific reasons such as unforeseen special events, competitor activity or natural disasters. Often the temptation exists to manually override allocations based on an inherent gut feel and this should be avoided at all costs.

The delivery instruction which is sent to the supplier specifies the quantities that must be picked and packed per item per store by colour and size.

The primary size refers to the commonly designated size of all products such as waist measurements, neck and chest sizes while the secondary size refers to products which have other options of the main primary size such as different leg lengths for trousers or varying cup size options in case of bras.

If automated replenishment systems do not exist or are not very sophisticated it may occur that the actual sales by size do not mirror those as planned. In such cases it is necessary to review the size patterns using a manual technique and alter contract ratios going forward. A special balancing contract must be raised for production of those specific sizes that are short in order to realign the size sales pattern to that of the amended regular contracts going forward. A very clear indication where the size ratio is out of line is where at the end of range launches the left over stocks or reduced stocks are dominated by one or two sizes. If one applies one's mind to the consequence of this, it is a fact that potential sales have gone drastically astray of better selling sizes and profit is consequently not maximised.

In summary, the sad part about poor performers or the lack of stock control, is that especially in the case of high volume continuity styles, the resultant negative impact can be likened to a lingering illness that lives with the buying team until the situation of overstocks of unwanted product is eventually rectified or doomed to the reduced counter. It is therefore critical that where there is a hint of such an evolving scenario that very swift action is taken.

Where there has been above average performance of categories, a situation may arise where the amount stock available is unable to satisfy the requirements of the entire store catalogue. In such instances the predicament that exists is one of how to keep everybody happy. The choice usually boils down to reducing the quantities proportionately across the entire catalogue dependent on the priority of need whereby at least each store sees a piece of the pie before sell outs are experienced. The other option is to take the view to shrink the number of stores that are serviced and best satisfy the stores that are more likely to deliver the greatest volume of sales. In many cases it is not uncommon for twenty percent of the catalogue to deliver sixty to seventy percent of the sales. The selection of the second option will retain the credibility of the customers in the bigger units but will disappoint the many customers across the balance of the stores. A tactic to alleviate severe situations is by choosing a geographical cross section of stores and if an on-line facility exists, to ensure that stock is available at all times that can be ordered via the internet.

The use of digital imaging has helped develop realistic three dimensional representations which enable the product to be placed efficiently on the various types of equipment in the store. Such systems operate at detail size level so in theory a store will never be out of a size as the principle applied is that as the store sells one it gets one. The key to the success of such a system is that the data integrity has to be as accurate as possible. If this is not the case, for example, where the data base is distorted through incorrect barcode ticketing or pilferage will result in allocations being calculated inaccurately. The only means to rectify the data base is to do a disciplined full manual stock count from time to time and update the data base accordingly.

The automatic replenishment or distribution of products is often performed through the use of sophisticated technical allocation systems and are most suitable for the basic continuity product that have consistent predictable sales patterns and for store displays which are laid out according to a centralised space planning system.

Delivery Instruction note example

ORDER NO	12345		DEPARTMENT	Men's Trousers	
SUPPLIER	ABC Manufacturer		STYLE NO	5554	
DATE	14 March, 2015		DESCRIPTION	Casual cotton trouser	

NO	STORE	COLOUR	GREY					
STORES		PRIMARY SIZE	32	34	36	38	40	42
		SECONDARY SIZE	32	34	36	38	40	42
NO	STORE	TOTAL	120	170	160	140	110	100
141	City Centre	250	38	53	50	44	34	66
145	Main Street	200	30	43	40	35	28	53
148	Back Street	250	38	53	50	44	34	66
151	Country Lane	100	15	21	20	18	14	26

PRODUCT STORAGE AND DISTRIBUTION

Logistical planning and supply chain

Supply chain logistics is described as the product movement comprising of the transport and shipment of goods from the point of origination and clearance through customs where applicable to the distribution centre or warehouse and on to stores where the goods are placed on offer for purchase to the customer. Many stores traditionally have stockroom facilities or at least a backroom to accommodate overflow stocks.

The reality is that the same rates of rental are charged as that for saleable metreage and therefore it is preferable that off-site storage facilities be maintained. The downside of holding stocks in high rental cost stock rooms is that invariably the remnant stocks of promotions or themes are removed from the sales floor and left in the stock room to gather dust waiting for the seasonal write down.

Out of season stocks such as thermal underwear are returned to the stockroom to await the reappearance of the next season to be returned to the sales floor. In such situations, particularly where there are undisciplined controls in the store, stocks get lost in the black hole of the stock room and bad or dead stock will accumulate and affect the data integrity of the stock records. It is therefore essential that redundant stocks are written off and cleared out almost immediately.

The trend is to keep store holding areas as small as possible and enable the regular drawing off from larger economical offsite storage facilities which can be done more effectively through a centralised point whether it be at the warehouse or in the commercial office. The success as to how well this is done is dependent on the responsiveness of the warehouse and reduces the accumulation of isolated pockets of stocks while minimising the corruption of stock data integrity as well as the reduction of double handling of merchandise.

Examples of stock held in the holding room is the accommodation of an overflow of stock where space planning is applied using planograms. End of ranges stock that have to be returned to the centralised storage facility or supplier may need to be held temporarily in the back room awaiting collection. Stock is also temporarily held for consolidation in back room areas until all components of a promotional launch is received and moved to the sales floor on the launch date for maximum impact.

The selection of the various options of supply chain will depend on a number of criteria such as the source of supply, characteristics of the product, the costs of the storage and distribution, selling locations, shelf life and customer demand.

The main channels of supply are a flow through model without storage or warehoused product. Outside of these channels the other formats are direct delivery to stores or displays being fully merchandised by the vendor.

The type of distribution model that is selected will depend on factors such as the size and growth phase of the retailer. For example, smaller or new retailers will probably prefer to operate a cross dock model which does not require investment in large warehouse facilities or the need to carry excessive inventory enabling their efforts to be focused possibly on opening more stores.

For a larger mature retail chain on the other hand, it may be essential to operate through a network of sophisticated warehousing amenities. These enjoy elaborate systems whereby they have better control of the management of the inventory and are able to efficiently allocate, pick and pack and schedule deliveries to stores country wide or even internationally.

Retailers also have the choice to manage their own facilities or outsource them. The main factor that is considered in selecting the most suitable option is the cost saving element. Initially it may have been cheaper to outsource without having to invest in the high setup cost of such an infra-structure, however, as the retailer grows, coupled to the fact that the third party is a profit based operation that delivers expertise in the warehousing field, the time will come when it is more beneficial to move the operation in house.

A workable compromise solution that is often employed is for the retailer to control their own warehouse facilities with the accompanying IT infrastructure and avoid the major upheaval should they change third parties but to still outsource the transport network part to specialised haulage service providers.

Cross dock or flow through model is the arrangement where the goods are pre picked and packed at the supplier and are delivered to the distribution centre with store labels already gummed on the boxes or hanging sets. The alternative model of cross dock is where the order across the stores is delivered in bulk by the supplier to the cross dock facility and the goods are picked by distribution centre staff and deposited directly in the respective store dispatch bays. Eventually the product from all suppliers for the day is consolidated in each store's designated bay awaiting transport.

Stores that are geographically far from the receiving distribution centre have the goods transhipped in bulk to their own respective closest geographical distribution centre where the picking operation will take place. The number of regional distribution centres will be largely dependent on the density of the store network and the operating costs of such facilities.

The added benefit of the goods being picked and packed at the supplier is that the cartons are able to contain a combination of size and colour requirements by store and will therefore eliminate the need to unpack and repack from warehouse stock thus eliminating double handling and is subsequently more cost efficient. It is also possible where the supplier is picking multiple styles for the same store that these can be nested in the same container which reduces the need for additional packaging as well as reduces handling making for a considerable time saving.

In the event that there are over or short deliveries these cause delays as the changed quantity requires that the computer is updated and the store quantities are scaled or recalculated based on varying algorithms that satisfy those stores with the greatest need first rather than simply apportioning equally across all the stores before the picking process can take place.

In the case where the receipt of product from suppliers is pre labelled for stores the testing of the accuracy is done by randomly inspecting a sample of cartons per supplier delivery and should the errors of packing fall outside of a certain tolerance it may result in the entire delivery being rejected. Where inaccuracies are within the tolerance but there is still a measure of incorrectness the error factor will still be extrapolated for the entire delivery and the invoicing is amended accordingly. Dependent on the size of the error it could attract a penalty. While many find this concept difficult to accept, it should be remembered that the time and cost to do a full unpack and reconciliation in all likelihood would render the operation to be considered impracticable. Tests have been statistically done which reveal that the deviation from the sample survey results is also not that large.

The advantage of a flow through supply chain type is that the allocation can be made as late as possible allowing the shortening of the lead time and thereby meeting the customer demand more efficiently. The other benefit is also that the storage space requirement is minimal and dependent on the payment obligation it may be beneficial to the retailer in terms of cash flow in that ownership is only transferred upon receipt at the distribution centre.

There is an argument that utilising cross dock without warehousing is possibly a disadvantage in terms of the speed of delivery to stores as having stock drawn from the warehouse is quicker and smoother than waiting for the supplier delivery. The challenge is therefore to streamline the supplier delivery efficiencies to avoid the cost impact of holding warehoused stock and the handling costs that accompany this option.

Other difficult situations arise where there is a poor performing unreliable supplier for which a contingency is required when they fail to deliver and similarly at key periods such as holidays where the factories shut down for a period and in spite of confirming that there will be a skeleton staff to cope with the execution of orders over this period the level of service is invariably diminished.

Example of a cross dock flow through model

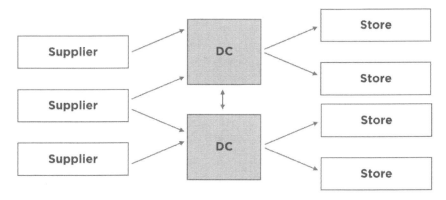

Warehoused product is where the goods are received in bulk and are held in storage awaiting a call off and distribution to stores or to other storage sheds using the cross dock facilities.

The warehouse can be seen to operate in a similar way as the supplier and performance management of indicators such as pick and pack accuracy, lead time measurement and the like can be implemented in the same way.

Warehoused stock tends to be predominantly for imported product but can also include local suppliers particularly where minimum order quantities or negotiated special volume deals apply. In the main the products are continuity items with long supply lead times which are replenished on a regular basis as "pull" allocations.

The challenge with warehouse stock is to manage the stock levels as the investment in high volumes does not only have adverse financial consequences but also a real physical problem can arise in the form of space constraints and the possible requirement of additional operational resources. There are also instances of seasonal goods such as knitwear being produced in the off season to maintain a consistent production throughout the year and therefore creates an accumulation of stocks in the warehouse either at the supplier or the retailer at a cost which needs to be accounted for.

A point to note is that the storage shelving location is restricted to a fixed size which is usually the size of a pallet and may be at multi levels. As goods are withdrawn to the pick and pack locations it does happen that within one storage location a lesser quantity of goods remain behind which results in the space utilisation not being optimal as two different SKU's are not able to share the same location. Technically the warehouse becomes restricted in the capacity availability while physically this may not be the case. Thought needs to be applied to the minimum percentage or quantity that is able to be efficiently maintained and what tactics must be utilised regarding the consolidation of and removal of such stocks to free up the storage slots. This may take the form of allocating the odds to stores or transferring it to a different storage area with smaller slots and take on a high priority for distribution thereafter.

Other space inhibiting practices are where there are poor rates of sales, or volume deals are negotiated or through minimum order quantities that are imposed which cause the warehouses to fill up eventually and consequently result in the total utilisation of palette slots. The alternative then remains to either source outside storage, put the brakes on in terms of accepting intake or to simply stop buying to relieve the space and financial strain. The consequences of this is that availabilities suffer with the disruption of the composition of product and theme launches as well as the service levels of suppliers decline when they put production on hold while they wait for the retailer's stock levels to diminish and inevitably will sell on to other competitors in order to keep their production capacity full and operational.

The siting and the number of warehouses will be reliant on the geographic network of stores, the proximity to suppliers and ports and will be dependent on the achievement of the most economical costs which need to be continually reviewed to ensure the delicate balance of viability is maintained. This balance is particularly important in the case of retail chains which continually open and close stores.

The introduction of higher levels of automation and the possibility of outsourcing operations to contractors or independent logistical organisations for storage and the management of the fleet of transport to tranship between storage points and schedule deliveries to stores also has an impact on the sustainability.

After the unloading of a container or truck at the back door, the cartons are consolidated and received, and then palletized for packing away in the storage facilities with unique identification location barcodes for ease of retrieval upon withdrawal in bulk.

After drawing product in bulk from the shelves the goods are moved to a pick and pack location to satisfy each stores order and are deposited in the unique store bays to await dispatch.

An alternative option is to pick and pack goods directly from storage shelves by store and when the order of the various products for each specific store is complete it is delivered to the store's relevant bay.

The appropriateness of which picking method to apply will depend largely on the size of the withdrawals. The larger volumes are usually removed to a picking area in bulk where the pick and pack operations take place. The smaller the quantities that are required by store, the picking by individual store across the product range into picking bins or shipping units for each store would probably be more suitable. It is possible that some retailer's employ both methods from different areas of the warehouse dependent on the product characteristics and volumes.

The task of picking is activated by the generation of a computer picking sheet which informs the picker as to which location must be accessed and indicates the quantity that must be withdrawn. Together with this the computer will create the store labels which is applied to the shipping container.

There are generally two methods of generating picking lists and labels. The more manual method is where the picking lists are generated up front prior to the picking operation but the downside is that it is susceptible to inaccuracies and at the end of the operation the computer needs to be updated manually and report any exceptions. The implication is that this step must be fulfilled before any goods can be shipped which could cause delays.

The other option is real time picking which is the technique of using hand held terminals that employ radio frequency to give the pickers their instructions on a computer terminal or pad. With the handheld terminal or voice instructions via hands free headsets the picker will scan the barcodes of the product and locations to confirm that the correct product has been identified and the picking can commence which will then update the stock data base in real time. For this reason the accuracy is almost guaranteed and the movement of stock is free flowing.

As all retailers are concerned about shrinkage this method is a big plus and also lessens the possibility of disputes between the warehouse and stores with respect to over or short deliveries. The facility to automatically generate store delivery notes is provided enabling the deliveries to be tracked. Real time control does however come at a much added cost and therefore the viability must be assessed in terms of the benefits it brings with it.

There are sophisticated automated picking systems which lessen the manual handling of product but these require a higher level of investment. The most common system employed is a conveyer belt system whereby the pickers are relatively stationery and are responsible for a section of products in an area where the items are packed onto the conveyer belt from which picking takes place and can be done for either the store or product picking options.

Challenges that the picking operation faces is that different approaches are required to segment activities in cases where fast selling items need to be picked more frequently and others such as for some stores that require less service than others. Consequently there is a prerequisite to carefully schedule actions in order to streamline deliveries.

In a similar way the peaks and valleys of volumes through the week apply undue strain on the operation at certain times while at other spells the warehouse may stand idle. In the case of clothing where there are not many expiry dates involved the approach should possibly be to pick the high volume product outside the peak delivery periods and reserve the ability to prioritise the promotion items during the peak delivery period thereby smoothing the operation and maintain a constant labour utilisation.

The ideal size of the warehouse is difficult to assess but the general rule is obviously the smaller the warehouse the better as the overheads are kept to a minimum and experience often shows whatever the size of the shed is it will inevitably be filled. The size should be tailored to the space required during normal trading and not to accommodate peak periods such as Christmas or the accumulation of stock build up prior to Chinese New Year when at

45

such times additional temporary space can possibly be procured or alternatively implement night shifts to keep stocks moving.

The flow of product within a warehouse environment is illustrated below

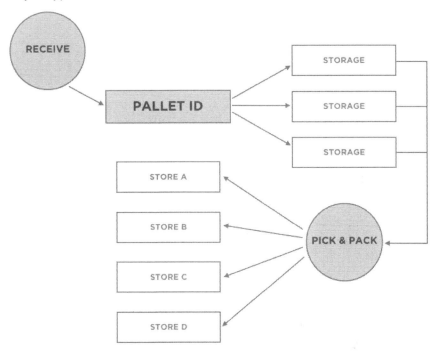

Direct delivery of product to the store location by the supplier is used where the retailer does not have the infrastructure to accommodate certain types of product such as high priced goods like cosmetics and expensive accessories.

This mode of delivery is also required where the vendor completes the end to end merchandising management of the displays whereby slow selling stock is withdrawn and replaced by the supplier. A typical example would be a product such as greeting cards, accessories and magazines.

In summary, a well-managed supply chain enables the retailer to acquire goods from the manufacturer more profitably, facilitate well controlled stock levels, and provide more timeous response to the consumer demand as well as the building of sustainable working relationships between the retailer and the supplier.

VALUE ADDED PROCESSING

The need for additional work on product is frequent and the facilities to do this has to be provided for to make goods store ready. The nature of value added work can take on a variety of forms but typical examples are as follows.

Goods that are received from off shore suppliers may be bulk packed or not be received in their final form in order to achieve optimum space utilisation during transit. Prime examples of this is in the case of cushions or duvets which are space hungry but are relatively light. In order to accomplish the most efficient space usage these goods may be transported without the fibre filling or alternatively are vacuum packed. However, this operation then creates the need for additional work upon receipt to fill the cushions and unpacking of the vacuum packs as well as treating the product through pressing or steaming.

The transport of goods in cartons that eventually will be displayed on hangers, such as men's formal suits or ladies tailored garments, is done to maximise the space efficiency in containers. Upon arrival they will need to be unpacked and placed on hangers and will have to be steamed either with a hand steamer or pass through a steam tunnel. In most cases this will also require the attachment of price tickets and garment information labels.

Repackaging may be required where bulk transit quantities need to be debagged and repackaged into smaller stock room packs ready for allocation to stores.

It does happen that there may be garments received from the supplier with defects or returned from stores which are repairable in order to make them available in a saleable state which has to be done by the value-adder.

The location of the added value service provider can be either at an independent site or be incorporated in the retailer's warehouse facility. The challenge with an offsite location, particularly with the receipt of offshore product is the fact that the goods are received by another facility and reflect on a separate stock record which renders the administration of stock to be more complex.

It is preferable to have the value added processing done in the retailer's warehouse facility as there is control of the receipt of the goods and performance is more easily managed. The operation can possibly be done on a contractual basis whereby the processor rents space within the warehouse or the space is alternatively staffed with warehouse resources as a separate entity and not included in the distribution centre operational costs. It should be noted that the cost of this processing work forms part of the cost of the product and must be included in the determination of the product margin.

The costing structures for work done is a complex one as the type of work is not always consistent and therefore needs to be broken down into some detail.

Value added costing would typically consist of a basic cost for the overheads and handling of the product which is usually relatively stable but may vary depending on the type of product being processed. Charges per operation such as a rate per garment for steaming, labelling, placing on hangers and the like will be added to the base costs. Out of the ordinary operations such as ad hoc repairs will be dependent on the results of negotiation between the processor and the buying departments.

TRANSPORT METHODOLOGIES

The method of transport will be determined by a number of criteria. The option for clothing is either in cartons or in the form of hanging sets. The choice is dependent mainly on the characteristic of the product, the cost comparison between the two models and the equipment infra-structure of the supplier and distribution centres. Many of the more sophisticated production plants have the overhead rail systems that can accommodate hanging goods and which can facilitate the transport of the goods hanging from rails affixed to the ceiling of the vehicle to the retailer.

The cost of the hanging storage and transport of product will come at added expense for the rail systems in comparison to the charge for distribution in cartons. The time saving as a cost offset in the case of moving hanging goods needs to be considered and in many cases it is also dependent on the nature of fabrics such as voiles as well as the structure of garments as is the case for formal wear. If crease sensitive goods are moved in cartons there is a need for an added value processing requirement to steam and bag the goods which can either take place at the distribution centre or at the stores upon receipt which comes at an additional cost. The transport of formal wear in cartons could also lead to persistent creases in the garment such as the fold in pants that may be difficult to eradicate even with intense steaming.

Where retailers insist on receiving goods in boxes, a reverse cost may have to be applied where sophisticated manufacturing plants that only cater for hanging goods to maximise the scales of efficiency will need to purchase cartons and employ additional labour to pack the garments into boxes as well as encounter an additional time delay.

The downsides of the hanging format is that the equipment is expensive, space requirement is greater, and where multiple hangers are hung vertically to save space in the outer bag there could be the danger of bunching of longer garments at the bottom of the bag. Space wastage below the hanging bags in the vehicles also needs to be taken into account.

The advantage of time saving that hanging formats deliver in comparison to goods transported in cartons is that goods in cartons have the benefit of easier handling, better space utilization and less capital investment. However the necessity of capacity planning for processing to steam and place products on hangers together with the additional cost, extended lead time and a risk that the quality may be compromised needs to be weighed up.

Another determining factor will be the aesthetics of the garment that may lend it to be displayed on hangers such as casual shirts made from natural fibres or styled tailored goods which will better highlight the features and promote the unique feel of the special fabrics.

Goods are stored and dispatched as hanging sets that will comprise of a fixed number of garments in the same colour and sizes and are allocated as such. This makes for easier handling and loading into vehicles especially where the equipment is able to access the vehicle or container directly from the despatch area.

The optimisation of the supply chain calls for an end to end cost analysis and monitoring to ensure that the goods reach the sales floors efficiently to best service the customer through consistent availability without the congestion of stock in warehouses and back rooms.

A flow diagram which indicates the garment and fibre types which best suit the method of storage, transport and display can be illustrated as follows

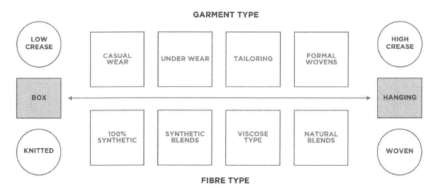

Product security

Wastage through pilferage is an important factor that needs attention during the movement of the product. Control is done by various methods but mostly through the use of sealed containers, marked sealing tapes on cartons, sample tests of contents in cartons, locked and sealed back doors on trucks and sophisticated handover procedures. There is a breakeven point where the cost to maintain the security must be weighed up against the shrinkage allowance as it may be overkill to secure cheaper products with refined protection. The additional labour and checkpoints will slow down the movement of product through the pipeline as well as lower the service levels and therefore may not make it meaningful. On the other hand it could well be very worthwhile for the movement of high value product.

Carton specifications and requirements

Transit and outer case cartons need to conform to certain specifications in terms of size, strength, weight, markings and sealing. The characteristics of certain products will dictate modifications to some cartons such as goods that are packed on hangers may require a tape at the ends inside the box to hook the hangers to prevent the shifting of product such as blouses within the cartons. Other products may require separators between the garments such as tissue paper or card board to minimise creasing.

Careful consideration must be given to the number of units per stockroom pack which will usually be by solid colour and solid size and should be equivalent to the unit of allocation. Savings can be achieved through less handling and storage configurations by setting the quantity per pack equivalent to the minimum allocation quantity that a store can accommodate without being overstocked.

Barcode markings enable the scanning in of boxes at the receipt points and alleviate the risk of congestion with less labour. Packing away on palettes into the storage slots is also done more quickly.

Markings on the cartons must be uniform and conform to international regulations and display a recognized certification stamp.

Side 1 marking required on the carton – product description

MARKING	DESCRIPTION
Retailer ABC	Name of the customer who is to take ownership of the product
Fragile	Indicates if the box should be handled with care
Supplier	Source of product where goods were supplied
Order no	Order that the box belongs to
Batch number	Production batch that carton belongs to
Product reference no	Style number of garments inside the box
SKU number	Stock keeping unit or barcode number that will be reflected on the stock records
Contents description	Style / colour / size and style description
Units per carton	Number of units inside the carton
Carton number	Number of carton out of the total (e.g. 'carton no 3 of 10')
Country of origin	Sending country (where carton was packaged)

Side 2 marking required on the carton – weight and measurement information

MARKING	DESCRIPTION
Fragile	Indicates if the box should be handled with care
Stack max	Maximum number of cartons that can be packed on top of each other
Net weight (kg)	Net weight in kg of goods inside the carton
Gross weight (kg)	Total weight of the outer carton and the goods inside the carton
Dimensions (cm or mm)	Dimensions of height, length and width of carton in cm or mm

Apart from conforming to international rules, the size parameters and volume dimensions will also be dictated by the pallette sizes and storage slots of the warehouse to safeguard the most efficient usage of space. The dimensions also need to be considered in terms of what the other equipment such as conveyer belts, vehicle capacities and store storage facilities can accommodate.

Carton critical measurements

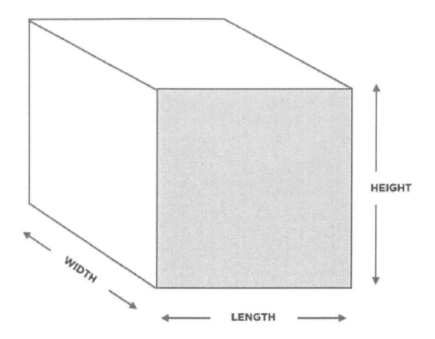

VOLUME = WIDTH X LENGTH X HEIGHT

Local logistics should investigate the possible use of returnable cartons or crates by suppliers much in the same way food retailers utilise lugs. Such an operation would be environmentally friendly and would incur a once off investment but the administration of such an operation does come at a cost which may influence the viability.

CONCLUSION

The book has tried to adequately describe in brief the key stakeholder's role in the process of retail fashion buying and planning and in particular the mechanisms and processes that then integrate with the logistical arm of the business and thereby highlight the options that are available to ensure that the product is secure and in a pristine condition when it is presented to the potential customer as an offer to purchase. Without the appropriate mechanisms and systems the entire effort of procuring the product and moving it to the point of sale could be all for nothing.

Printed in Great Britain
by Amazon